# The Case for Common Sense: Why Far-Left 'Extremism' Deserves a Hearing

Vanida Plamondon

While every precaution has been taken in the preparation of this book, the publisher assumes no responsibility for errors or omissions, or for damages resulting from the use of the information contained herein.

THE CASE FOR COMMON SENSE: WHY FAR-LEFT 'EXTREMISM' DESERVES A HEARING

First edition. November 7, 2024.



ISBN: 979-8227695017

Written by Vanida Plamondon.

# The Case for Common Sense: Why Far-Left 'Extremism' Deserves a Hearing

When people hear the word "extremist," they usually think of images that make them uncomfortable, far-right rallies, hate groups, and violent uprisings. It's a term loaded with judgment, and honestly, it's understandable. Extremism, in the context of the far right, often means disregarding fundamental human rights, nurturing hate, and enforcing rigid hierarchies that harm anyone not fitting into narrow definitions of "acceptable." Far-right "extremism" has tainted the term so profoundly that now, just saying you're on the "far" end of anything is practically a confession. But what if we just looked at what it means instead of demonizing the word and applied it fairly?

To me, the core idea of being a far-left "extremist" isn't about disruption for its own sake or forcing any particular lifestyle on anyone. It's about understanding that the current system fails many people and recognizing that a severe and honest shift is necessary. If I believe that shelter, food, healthcare, and education are human rights, why does that make me "extreme?" Why is it considered out of bounds to argue that our institutions should be held accountable to the public, not just their shareholders or political allies? Just because the values I advocate don't neatly fit within our society's status quo doesn't mean they're dangerous or destructive. They're constructive; they're meant to build systems that work for most people, especially those currently marginalized.

The difference between the far-right and far-left "extremes" really couldn't be more apparent, yet they get lumped together constantly. The far-right seeks to hoard resources, preserve privilege, and shut down opportunities for people who don't fit their mould. In their vision, we keep a hierarchy that's always worked well for a few at the top but limits freedom, diversity, and compassion. In contrast, the far-left pushes for universal access to essentials like housing, food, and health. Our policies aren't built on excluding people, but on expanding security and opportunity so no one is left out. So, to me, it seems like the term "extremist" actually loses meaning when we apply it to both far-left and far-right ideas. If "extreme" simply means pushing for something far from what exists today, then yes, I'll own the term, but let's also acknowledge that there's a world of difference in our goals and methods.

Being a far-left "extremist" simply means I'm unwilling to settle for a society that lets people fall through the cracks. I want a system where companies can't turn a profit by withholding life-saving drugs or where people's lives don't fall apart because they can't afford an essential hospital visit. That kind of economic inequality isn't just unfortunate; it's designed to keep the power with those who already have it. When people hear "extreme," they imagine something unstable, maybe even reckless. But what if the most stable, compassionate society is one that takes a hard stand against inequality? What if refusing to accept today's broken status quo is actually the most common-sense thing we can do?

This stigma around "extremism" ends up working to protect the interests of those who benefit from the current system, whether they realize it or not. The fear of anything far-left blocks real solutions before they can even be heard. However, we need new ideas that address people's real concerns, not in abstract terms but in actual, life-changing policies. So yes, if that's what it means to be a far-left "extremist," I'll wear the label proudly. The only difference is that my "extreme" isn't about division or hate; it's about giving people the essentials they need to live dignified, fulfilling lives. Maybe that's not so extreme after all.

# 'Extremism' In Light Of Structural Challenges

When we think about what's considered "extreme" today, it's surprising how much of it is just a reaction to problems that have gone unaddressed for too long. We're living in a world where income inequality is staggering, the climate crisis is accelerating, and millions of people can't afford a place to live. But talk about significant, structural changes to fix these things, and suddenly, you're labelled an "extremist." This idea that seeking real solutions is "too radical" only makes sense if you ignore the scope of the challenges we're up against. So maybe it's time to redefine what we mean by "extreme" and recognize that many of the so-called radical ideas we're talking about are, in reality, necessary responses to genuine issues.

Take inequality, for instance. We're constantly told that it's just "how the system works" and that some people will always be rich, and others will struggle. But when you look at the numbers, you see that wealth isn't just spread unevenly; it's hoarded by a tiny fraction of people, often at the expense of the majority. In what world does it make sense that a handful of billionaires have as much wealth as half the population? Yet, suggest policies that would rebalance this, like progressive taxation or strong labour protections, and you're branded as having extreme views. The real extremism, if you ask me, is a system that allows a few people to accumulate absurd wealth while so many are barely getting by. By reframing "extreme" to mean the policies that ignore this inequality, we start to see that those who defend the status quo are actually the ones with the radical stance.

Climate change is another structural challenge that forces us to reconsider what's extreme. We're facing a global crisis affecting every aspect of life on this planet, yet meaningful action still gets stalled because people are afraid of "disrupting the economy." The irony is that if we don't disrupt how things are going, there won't be much of an economy to worry about. The consequences of doing nothing are already here, from wildfires and hurricanes to droughts and rising sea levels. Still, the mainstream view clings to incremental changes, suggesting we should "recycle more" instead of pushing corporations to overhaul their environmental practices. We're told that system-wide changes to address climate change, like renewable energy transitions and carbon taxes, are too extreme. But when you think about it, ignoring the planet's limits and continuing business as usual seems far more radical, even reckless. Reframing the conversation around climate action as common sense rather than extreme highlights just how far we need to shift our priorities if we're going to have a future at all.

Then there's the housing crisis. Right now, housing has turned into a high-stakes investment game where developers and landlords make massive profits. At the same time, regular people can barely afford rent, let alone own a home. Housing prices have skyrocketed in cities worldwide, and wages just haven't kept up. The mainstream solutions we hear usually focus on "increasing supply" by building more luxury apartments or giving tax breaks to developers, as if that will magically make rents affordable. But people call it extreme when you bring up ideas like public housing, rent control, or co-op models that take profit out of the equation. Why is it so out there to say that housing should be about sheltering people, not lining investors' pockets? Calling these solutions "extreme" doesn't reflect their actual impact; it just reinforces the current system, which is already failing millions. By redefining extreme in the context of housing, we acknowledge that the real problem isn't bold solutions; it's the idea that housing can remain a commodity in a world where people struggle to afford a place to live.

These issues have in common that they're structural challenges that won't be solved by minor tweaks or halfway measures. Inequality, climate change, and housing aren't just "problems"; they're symptoms of a system designed in ways that concentrate wealth and power. Labelling any serious challenge to this system as "extreme" avoids the uncomfortable truth that we need real change, not just adjustments. Redefining extreme isn't about embracing radicalism for its own sake; it's about recognizing that the most significant risks we face are in maintaining a status quo that's clearly unsustainable.

# Regulation, Equity, And Public Welfare

When I talk about regulation, equity, and public welfare, I'm really talking about building a society that can handle whatever gets thrown its way. We're facing constant challenges, whether economic instability, climate disasters, or rising inequality, and we need systems that work for us, not against us. So, let's start with regulation. People often hear the word and think it means bureaucracy or red tape, but good regulation is about setting up guardrails so that companies and markets don't run roughshod over people and the environment. It's like the saying, "An ounce of prevention is worth a pound of cure." Regulations are meant to prevent the worst and protect us from financial crashes, environmental damage, and exploitation. It's not about stifling growth or innovation; it's about making sure those things happen to benefit everyone, not just the top 1%.

Equity is another crucial piece of the puzzle. In a world as interconnected as ours, leaving people behind isn't just unfair; it's unsustainable. When we talk about equity, we're talking about creating systems that recognize people's different starting points in life. It's about levelling the playing field so that everyone has a fair chance, no matter where they come from or what resources they were born with. Equity is what helps communities thrive. Imagine a society where access to education, healthcare, and safe housing isn't a privilege but a given for everyone. That kind of fairness doesn't just make life better for individuals; it builds a stronger, more resilient society because people aren't weighed down by avoidable hardships. Equity gives everyone a stake in the system and a reason to contribute precisely what you want in a stable, healthy society.

Public welfare, meanwhile, is about ensuring a baseline quality of life for everyone. It's strange to me that people think of public welfare as something "radical" when it's common sense. Suppose we ensure everyone can access healthcare, education, and social support. In that case, we're creating a population that can weather hard times together. Public welfare isn't charity or a handout; it's an investment in resilience. When people aren't constantly worried about falling through the cracks, they're more likely to contribute positively to society, innovate, and support others. Think about it: a society where people know they'll be taken care of if they lose their jobs or get sick is one where people feel empowered to take risks, start businesses, or support each other without fear. In this way, public welfare isn't just a safety net; it's a foundation for a resilient, forward-looking society.

Regulation, equity, and public welfare aren't about restricting freedom or going "soft" on people. They're about creating a balanced system that can withstand challenges and adapt over time. These themes aren't just about survival; they're about building a prepared society. When we design our systems with resilience, we're setting ourselves up to thrive, no matter what the future holds. That's not "extreme." It's just practical.

# Unregulated Capitalism

Unregulated capitalism is often sold to us as the system that drives innovation, promotes freedom, and delivers prosperity. But when you peel back the surface, you start to see that it has a pretty poor track record for meeting people's essential needs. Take housing, for instance. In a system where profit is the primary goal, housing becomes just another investment, a way for the wealthy to make money rather than a fundamental right for everyone. We're seeing more and more people priced out of their neighbourhoods, forced into unaffordable rents, or left without stable shelter altogether. Developers focus on luxury units because that's where the profits are, while affordable housing becomes scarce. And when the market is left to its own devices, there's no real incentive to change that dynamic. If unregulated capitalism worked for housing, millions wouldn't struggle to keep a roof over their heads.

Healthcare is another area where unregulated capitalism falls short and impacts everyone. In a profit-driven system, healthcare is often about maximizing revenue instead of focusing on patient well-being. We see this in outrageous drug prices, limited access to essential services, and insurance companies deciding who does and doesn't get care based on their bottom line. The idea is that competition will lower prices and improve quality, but that hasn't happened. Instead, healthcare costs have risen, quality of care is uneven, and people avoid going to the doctor because they can't afford it. The thing is, when your health is at risk, you shouldn't have to worry about whether or not you can pay. But that's precisely what happens in a system without regulation to prioritize access and affordability.

Even something as essential as food isn't immune from the pitfalls of unregulated capitalism. Our entire industry is focused on cheap production and maximizing profits, often at the cost of quality and nutrition. In low-income areas, people are left with "food deserts" where there's hardly any access to fresh, nutritious food. Meanwhile, profit-driven fast-food chains and processed food companies flood the market with cheap, unhealthy options. It's a system that incentivizes quantity over quality, and it's one where the population's health takes a back seat. Suppose capitalism were really meeting our needs in this area. In that case, we'd see everyone with access to fresh, affordable, and nutritious food, but that's far from the reality.

Jobs are supposed to be a major "benefit" of capitalism, but even here, the system's flaws show through. In unregulated markets, companies are driven to maximize profit by any means, often cutting wages, eliminating benefits, and offering little job security. Workers are treated as costs to be minimized rather than people whose well-being should be supported. And while we're told that a "free market" encourages businesses to offer competitive wages to attract talent, many people are barely scraping by without strong labour laws or minimum wage requirements. Corporations focus on short-term profits for their shareholders. In the process, they strip down jobs to their bare minimums, leaving people exhausted, underpaid, and without basic benefits. If unregulated capitalism could meet our essential need for stable, fair-paying work, we wouldn't need to constantly debate things like minimum wage increases or fighting for healthcare benefits in the workplace.

At the end of the day, unregulated capitalism just isn't designed to meet essential human needs. It's set up to prioritize profit, and when that becomes the sole focus, people get left behind. The gaps we see in housing, healthcare, food access, and job stability aren't accidental. They're the natural outcomes of a system that values profits over people and isn't equipped to address society's core needs.

# Unregulated Capitalism Fails Society

It's funny how often I'm told that my views are "too extreme," considering that a lot of research actually backs up what I'm saying about unregulated capitalism failing society. Study after study has shown that when markets are left unchecked, it's not prosperity that spreads but inequality. Let's start with income inequality, one of the clearest examples of how the free market doesn't naturally balance itself out. Research shows that, over time, wealth tends to concentrate at the top unless we have strong policies to redistribute it. Without intervention, the rich get richer, and the gap keeps growing. This isn't just a fluke or a "side effect"; it's a pattern we consistently see when capitalism runs without any meaningful regulation. The idea that wealth will "trickle down" if we just let businesses operate freely sounds nice. Still, it doesn't hold up under scrutiny.

Then there's the impact of unregulated capitalism on healthcare, and the numbers are pretty damning here, too. Studies comparing healthcare systems worldwide show that countries with heavily regulated, often publicly funded systems end up with better health outcomes and lower costs per capita than the predominantly private, profit-driven system in the U.S. Research shows how the U.S., despite its massive spending, has worse health outcomes in terms of life expectancy, infant mortality, and preventable diseases. The profit motive, it turns out, doesn't prioritize patient care. Instead, it encourages high prices, limited access, and inequality in who gets treated. When the focus is on maximizing revenue, the system ends up serving shareholders more than it serves patients, and research consistently shows that this approach fails to meet the healthcare needs of society as a whole.

The housing market tells a similar story. Research has shown that, in unregulated markets, housing prices skyrocket, leading to shortages of affordable homes and increased homelessness. For example, cities that have taken a more laissez-faire approach have seen housing costs spiral out of control because the market prioritizes luxury developments for those who can afford them. Research from places that have tried rent control or public housing investment shows that regulations can make a huge difference in keeping housing affordable for everyday people. So when people say "the market will fix it," the data says otherwise. Without intervention, housing becomes less about shelter and more about investment, which is good for some but disastrous for many.

Even on the environment, research aligns with the so-called "extreme" view that capitalism needs boundaries. Studies on environmental degradation and climate change make it clear that profit-driven industries left unchecked have been major drivers of pollution and resource depletion. The fossil fuel industry, for example, has known about the effects of carbon emissions for decades. Still, without regulation, they had no incentive to change. Researchers have shown that the most effective way to reduce emissions isn't through voluntary action or hoping companies will "do the right thing" but through adequate regulation, carbon taxes, and public investment in green technologies. The science on this is pretty solid; if we want to tackle climate change, we need strong policies that push industries to act responsibly, not a system that lets them chase profits no matter the cost.

Unregulated capitalism, when examined through the lens of research, has a clear pattern: it serves those at the top, often at the expense of everyone else. Studies on labour markets, too, show that without regulations like minimum wage laws or protections for workers, wages stagnate while productivity and corporate profits increase. As economists have documented, this "decoupling" of productivity from wages shows that a booming economy doesn't necessarily mean better lives for the workers who drive it. The idea that a rising tide lifts all boats just doesn't hold up when you look at the data; it's more like a rising tide lifts the yachts while everyone else gets a leak in their boat.

While some may call my views "extreme," I see them as grounded in evidence. Research backs up the need for regulations and policies that prioritize people's health, housing, wages, and environment over unchecked corporate profits. The data shows us that unregulated capitalism fails to deliver basic needs for the majority, so maybe it's time to admit that what I'm proposing isn't extreme; it's just common sense backed by facts.

# Capitalist Entities Should Become Responsible, Contributing Citizens

When I say I believe in complete regulation of capitalism, I'm not saying I want to shut down businesses or eliminate the profit motive altogether. Instead, I'm saying that if capitalist entities are going to operate within society, they should have responsibilities just like everyone else. I believe capitalism doesn't have to be a free-for-all where anything goes as long as a profit is made. It can and should be a system where businesses operate responsibly, benefiting society instead of just themselves. My so-called "extremist" view isn't anti-capitalist; it's about making capitalism work for people. I argue that businesses, especially those that profit significantly from society's resources and infrastructure, must give back and contribute meaningfully.

Think about it: we already expect individuals to be responsible citizens, pay taxes, obey laws, and contribute to the common good. So why should it be any different for corporations? These companies benefit from public resources like infrastructure, legal protections, and an educated workforce, all things our tax dollars help fund. Isn't it fair to expect them to contribute to the society they're profiting from? In my mind, regulation isn't about restricting businesses for the sake of it; it's about setting up a framework that ensures companies are held accountable to the people who support them, whether directly or indirectly.

One of the most significant ways businesses can contribute is by treating their workers fairly. Believing that people deserve decent pay, safe working conditions, and job security is not radical. Yet, without regulations, we've seen that many companies cut corners in these areas to maximize profit. This isn't just unfair to workers; it's unsustainable. When companies underpay employees, those workers rely on social programs to make ends meet. This is ironic because it means taxpayers subsidize companies' low wages. Regulating labour practices so that companies provide fair wages and benefits isn't about punishing businesses; it's about ensuring that they take on their fair share of responsibility for the workforce they rely on. Suppose we want to build a robust and resilient society. In that case, we can't allow businesses to exploit workers and then shift the burden to the public when those workers struggle.

The environment is another area where I think responsible capitalism should shine. Suppose a company is profiting from natural resources or emitting pollution. In that case, they should be held accountable for the environmental impact they create. Right now, many companies treat the environment as an unlimited resource and dump waste without a second thought because it saves money. However, this "profit at any cost" approach is dangerous when dealing with climate change and resource depletion. Regulation here isn't about stifling growth; it's about ensuring growth doesn't come at the planet's expense. By enforcing emissions, waste disposal, and sustainable resource use standards, we can ensure that businesses contribute to the common good rather than degrade it. Responsible capitalism should mean a commitment to sustainability, where companies understand that short-term gains shouldn't come at the expense of long-term planetary health.

Taxation, too, is an essential part of making capitalism responsible. Right now, we see massive corporations using loopholes to avoid paying taxes despite benefiting immensely from the society around them. This isn't just a "smart business practice"; it's a failure of responsibility. Taxes fund the public services and infrastructure that businesses depend on, from roads and schools to legal protections and emergency services. By dodging taxes, companies are effectively taking without giving back. Why should corporations be any different if we expect regular citizens to pay their taxes? A well-regulated tax system ensures that companies contribute fairly to the society they profit from, making them active participants in the welfare of their communities.

My idea of regulating capitalism is about raising the bar for what we expect from businesses. It's about creating a system where companies aren't just profit-driven entities but also responsible citizens who play a positive role in society. This isn't about being anti-business; it's about being pro-responsibility. When we hold businesses accountable, we're not restricting them but empowering them to be better and more sustainable. We're saying that capitalism can be part of the solution instead of part of the problem, but only if we put adequate regulations in place to ensure it serves everyone, not just a few at the top.

# Government-Managed Housing

I get that government-managed housing might sound like an "extreme" idea to some people. But when you break it down, it's one of the most practical and effective ways to tackle housing insecurity. In many places, we see that the private market isn't equipped to provide affordable housing for everyone. The profit-driven model pushes developers toward building luxury units because they're the most lucrative, leaving a massive gap in affordable options. So, when I talk about government-managed housing or crown corporations for housing, I'm not saying private housing should disappear; we need a solid, stable option that prioritizes people's right to shelter over profit.

Government-managed housing offers something the private market just can't: stability. By involving public agencies in housing, we create a system that doesn't have to answer to shareholders or constantly worry about profit margins. Instead, its mission can be simple, make sure everyone has a place to live. That's the kind of steady, grounded approach we need if we're going to address housing insecurity. When the government steps in as a provider, it can set rent prices based on what people can afford, not what the market can bear. And in cities that have embraced models like this, it works. People there don't see public housing as a last resort or a marker of poverty; they see it as a viable, even desirable, option that takes the pressure off an overheated market.

Another significant advantage of government-managed housing is the long-term affordability it can provide. One of the biggest problems with the current market is that rents keep increasing.

Even if someone finds a place they can afford today, there's no guarantee they'll be able to stay there in a year or two if the landlord decides to raise the rent. With government-managed housing, rent increases can be controlled to match income growth and inflation rather than whatever the highest bidder is willing to pay. It creates a layer of security for people, knowing they won't be priced out of their homes just because the neighbourhood suddenly becomes more popular or profitable. This stability benefits communities, too, as people are more likely to invest in their neighbourhoods when they know they can afford to stay.

And it's not just about rent prices; government-managed housing can also ensure that buildings are actually maintained. In many private rentals, landlords cut corners or delay repairs to save money, and renters have little power to demand better. In a government-run system, there's accountability. The government is vested in keeping these buildings in good shape because it's a public service, not just a source of income. Well-maintained housing means people live in safer, healthier environments, and it builds trust in the system. When people see that their housing is prioritized, they know their well-being is valued.

A crown corporation model for housing also allows for innovation in how we design and structure our communities. Instead of cramming in as many units as possible for the highest price, government-managed housing can prioritize livability, green spaces, and community resources. Imagine housing developments designed for maximum efficiency and quality of life, places with playgrounds, community centers, and easy access to public transportation. A publicly funded system could prioritize sustainable, energy-efficient buildings, which benefit everyone by reducing carbon emissions and lowering utility costs for residents. Private developers rarely have these kinds of priorities. Still, a government-managed system can think beyond profit and create spaces serving the community in the long run.

The idea of government-managed housing might seem like overreach. Still, the reality is that our current approach just isn't working for a considerable portion of the population. Relying solely on the private market has literally left too many people out in the cold. The need for affordable, stable housing will not disappear. Until we're willing to consider solutions that might seem "radical," we'll keep running into the same problems. Government-managed housing is one of the few ways to ensure housing remains affordable and accessible, even in cities where property values skyrocket. That's not extreme; it's just common sense for a society that values stability, fairness, and the basic dignity of a secure home.

# Food Production And Distribution

It might sound "extreme" to some people. Still, I genuinely believe that government-led food production and distribution initiatives are essential for addressing the systemic issues that contribute to food insecurity. We've all heard the arguments about how the free market will take care of food production and distribution independently. Still, the reality is far more complicated and much darker than that. Right now, we live in a system where access to healthy, nutritious food is tied directly to one's income, location, and sometimes even social status. This isn't just an inconvenience; it's a structural problem that perpetuates inequality and causes actual harm to people's health and well-being. The current system isn't built to feed everyone but to make a profit. And when profit is the primary motivator, too many people are left behind.

When we leave food production to private companies, the emphasis is maximizing efficiency and profits, not ensuring equitable access to healthy food. Large corporations dominate the food supply chain, often driving prices up or creating a system where food is cheap but nutritionally bankrupt. Take a walk through many low-income neighbourhoods, and you'll see food deserts, areas where access to fresh, affordable produce is almost nonexistent, and cheap, unhealthy processed food is the only option available. This isn't a coincidence; it results from a system prioritizing profit margins over people's health. In an unregulated system, food becomes just another commodity to buy and sell for the highest price. Meanwhile, those who can't afford it are left scrambling, often relying on emergency food programs that aren't enough to address the underlying issue of food insecurity.

This is where I believe government-led initiatives can make a real difference. If we treated food as a fundamental human right, which everyone should have access to, regardless of income level or zip code, it would shift the entire system. The government could ensure that food is produced, distributed, and priced in ways that prioritize public health over private profit. We could establish systems where locally grown, healthy food is accessible to everyone, not just those who can afford the premium price tags in upscale grocery stores. By taking food production and distribution under public control, we could focus on sustainable practices that promote health, reduce waste, and ensure equitable access. This isn't about eliminating all private agriculture or food businesses but ensuring the government provides an option that puts people's well-being first.

Moreover, public food initiatives could provide the infrastructure and support necessary to improve local food systems. Most small farmers and food producers struggle to compete with massive agribusinesses. Still, with the right public policies, we could help support healthier local food systems for people and the environment. Imagine community-run food hubs that allow farmers to sell directly to consumers, cutting out the intermediaries who take a considerable chunk of the profits. Imagine a network of public food distribution centers that ensure low-income families have access to healthy food without relying on charity or paying exorbitant prices. This is what a government-led approach to food production and distribution could look like, shifting the focus from making money to ensuring the health and stability of all people.

The harm caused by food insecurity is not just about hunger; it's about the ripple effects of poor nutrition. Studies have shown that people who can't access nutritious food are more likely to develop chronic diseases like diabetes, heart disease, and obesity. These conditions lead to higher medical costs, lost productivity, and a lower quality of life for individuals, which strains public health systems. Suppose we want to truly address the societal harm caused by food insecurity. In that case, we must look beyond just getting people food when hungry. We need to fix the systems that are keeping people hungry in the first place. That means ensuring everyone has access to food that fills their stomachs and nourishes their bodies. A government-led approach could prioritize this kind of long-term, holistic thinking.

It's easy to dismiss government intervention as "extreme." Still, when you look at the scale of the issue, the need for fundamental change is undeniable. The current food system isn't just inefficient; it's harming people and contributing to broader societal problems. Introducing government-led food production and distribution initiatives could lead to a more equitable system that ensures everyone has access to the healthy, affordable food they need to thrive. This isn't about radical socialism; it's about taking responsibility for a system that affects everyone. If that's "extreme," then maybe it's time we rethink what radical means.

# Crown Corporations In Food Sectors

I firmly believe crown corporations in the food sector could be crucial in enhancing food security and quality. The idea of government-run food production and distribution may raise eyebrows. Still, when we look at the bigger picture, it's clear that relying solely on the private market to meet our food needs is not cutting it, especially for those who are most vulnerable. Right now, the food industry is dominated by large corporations that are more interested in maximizing profits than providing equitable access to healthy, affordable food. The result is a system where nutritious food is either out of reach for many or doesn't even exist in the neighbourhoods that need it most. If we put crown corporations in charge of certain aspects of food production and distribution, we could create a system where food is treated as a public good, not just a commodity.

Let's be clear: I'm not advocating for a complete government takeover of the food sector, but rather the establishment of publicly-run food systems that complement and regulate the existing market. The goal isn't to shut down private businesses but to provide a stable, affordable alternative for those left behind. For example, crown corporations could operate in areas like grain production, dairy, or even local food distribution, ensuring a consistent and reliable supply of affordable, healthy food for everyone. By taking these essential sectors under public management, we could stabilize prices, guarantee fair wages for workers, and ensure that the focus is on quality and sustainability, not just short-term profit margins.

Crown corporations could also create a system where local farmers are supported rather than exploited. Currently, many small-scale farmers struggle to compete with massive agribusinesses controlling the food supply chain. Integrating small-scale, sustainable farming into a public system could prioritize regional food production, reduce transportation costs, and create more resilient, local food systems. This would benefit both farmers and consumers. Crown corporations could work to ensure that local products are reasonably priced, reducing the monopoly large corporations have over what's grown, how it's priced, and where it's sold. Instead of being squeezed by corporate interests, small farmers could thrive in a system that supports their work, ensuring a diverse, healthy food supply.

Additionally, crown corporations in the food sector would allow the government to prioritize food quality and safety over profit. Much of our food is processed and filled with additives, preservatives, and chemicals that extend shelf life but don't always nourish our bodies. With government involvement in food production, we could demand higher standards for nutrition and health. Publicly run systems could focus on growing organic, non-GMO crops and ensuring sustainable food production practices, minimizing environmental harm. Unlike private corporations, which often cut corners to reduce costs, a crown corporation could invest in practices prioritizing long-term health for people and the planet.

Moreover, government-managed food systems could be vital in addressing food insecurity in marginalized communities. Many low-income areas are food deserts, with limited or nonexistent access to fresh produce. With a crown corporation overseeing food distribution, the government could ensure that healthy food is available where it's needed most, at prices that people can afford. Instead of relying on charity programs or non-profits to fill the gap, a well-run public system could ensure consistent, reliable access to nutritious food. This kind of stability is essential in times of crisis, like during natural disasters or economic downturns when private businesses often reduce services or increase prices to protect their profits. On the other hand, a crown corporation could serve as a stable food provider regardless of market conditions.

All of this doesn't mean that private food companies would disappear. I'm not anti-business; I'm anti-inequity and inefficiency. The goal isn't to eliminate the market but to ensure that the basic human need for food is met with dignity, sustainability, and fairness. Crown corporations in the food sector could work alongside private businesses to enhance overall food security. The public sector can set the standard for a just and sustainable food system, and private companies can continue innovating and competing within those boundaries. In this way, the government's role would be to ensure that everyone, regardless of income, background, or zip code, has access to healthy food while fostering an economy that's less dependent on the whims of the market.

It is not actually "extreme" to argue for crown corporations in the food sector to enhance food security and quality. It's about using the governance tools to ensure that our food system works for the many, not just the few. Publicly run food systems would provide a stable and sustainable food supply. Still, they would also hold the market accountable for its role in public health. By embracing this approach, we can create an equitable, healthy, and secure food system. This idea should be celebrated, not dismissed as extreme.

# Public Ownership Of Utilities And Insurance

It blows my mind how it's considered "extreme" to argue for public ownership of utilities and insurance, especially when these are two of the most basic necessities people rely on. The idea that essential services like electricity, water, heating, and even insurance should be run for profit is not just bizarre; it's a recipe for exploitation. And yet, somehow, the very suggestion that these things should be managed publicly to ensure fairness and prevent price-gouging is branded as "radical" or "extremist." But if we're honest with ourselves, is it really extreme to think everyone should have access to these essential services without being bankrupted by them? Because to me, it sounds like common sense.

Look at utilities, for instance. Electricity, water, heating, gas, these aren't luxuries, they're things people need to live. And yet, in many parts of the world, they are run by private companies whose sole interest is making money. What does that mean for consumers? It means rising prices, reduced service quality, and a growing number of people who simply can't afford to pay their bills. How can we sit back and pretend this is okay? If we leave essential services to the private sector, there will always be a disconnect between the needs of the people and the bottom line of the companies providing those services. For example, utility companies often charge sky-high prices during periods of high demand, effectively price-gouging people who have no choice but to pay. The same happens when natural disasters hit, and companies jack up the cost of goods like bottled water or gasoline. Public ownership of these services would stop that, ensuring prices remain affordable, even during a crisis. Isn't that precisely the kind of protection we should expect from our government?

The argument against public ownership usually comes down to the fear of "big government" or the supposed inefficiency of the public sector. But when you look at the facts, these arguments don't hold water. When public services are run well, they're far more reliable and accessible than their private counterparts. Take the example of public healthcare systems. These systems provide universal access to healthcare, funded through taxes, without the exorbitant costs and limitations imposed by private insurance companies. Utilities can operate similarly, funded by public dollars and administered to provide service to everyone, not just those who can afford to pay. When the government manages these services, it can keep prices stable, invest in infrastructure, and ensure that people have access regardless of income level. The idea that public systems are automatically less efficient is outdated. It doesn't consider the fundamental flaws of privatized systems that put profit over people.

Insurance is another area where public ownership could make a huge difference. Insurance companies are notorious for denying claims, hiking premiums, and finding ways to limit coverage to maximize their profits. This creates a system where people are forced to pay into something they might never get anything out of. When they need it most, the coverage is minimal or nonexistent. Health insurance, car insurance, and home insurance are all things people rely on to protect their well-being and security, but under a private, profit-driven model, the goal is not to provide protection; it's to make money. Publicly run insurance programs could eliminate this conflict of interest. Instead of operating with an eye on maximizing shareholder profits, public insurance would operate to provide real coverage and protection to everyone, regardless of their income level. This would create a more equitable and sustainable system where people could rely on the protection they've been promised and not have to fight tooth and nail to get it.

The fear that public ownership somehow means inefficiency or mismanagement doesn't hold up when we consider the damage that unregulated private industries cause. We've seen how private utility companies gouge customers with exorbitant fees or how insurance companies refuse coverage or inflate premiums. These industries have repeatedly proven that their interests don't align with the well-being of the people they serve. And yet, despite this track record, the idea of bringing these industries into the public sector is still treated as "extremist." But why is it extreme to suggest that people should be able to access life's essentials without being financially crippled? The real extremism is in allowing private companies to hold essential services hostage, put their profits above people's needs, and systematically create a situation where only the wealthy can afford the things we all depend on.

Public ownership isn't about abolishing private industry or removing competition where it makes sense; it's about recognizing that some services are too essential to be left to the whims of the market. Whether it's utilities, insurance, or other vital services, the public sector can ensure everyone has access at fair prices and high-quality service. If that's considered extreme, then I'm all for it. Because when it comes to the basic needs that people depend on, common sense should always trump profit.

# Public Goods, Improve National Stability And Equality

It's baffling to me that treating basic amenities like healthcare, education, housing, and utilities as public goods is considered "radical." How did it become so extreme to believe that everyone benefits when we treat fundamental needs as rights? The truth is that ensuring everyone has access to basic necessities is one of the best ways to improve national stability and equality. When people don't have to worry about whether they can afford healthcare or a place to live, they have more freedom to pursue opportunities, contribute to society, and live healthier, more fulfilling lives. This isn't radical; it's basic common sense, yet somehow, it's seen as a far-left fantasy.

Look at any society where basic amenities are treated as public goods. You'll see better outcomes in terms of social stability. In countries with universal healthcare, for example, people are less likely to go bankrupt because of medical bills, less likely to skip necessary treatments because they can't afford them, and more likely to live longer, healthier lives. That's not just a win for individuals; it's a win for society. When people are healthy, they can work, care for their families, and participate fully in their communities. It creates a ripple effect that improves productivity, reduces crime, and boosts well-being. How is this "radical" when it's clearly beneficial for everyone?

The same logic applies to housing. Housing is often framed as a "privilege" in a capitalist society, but it should be a right. When people don't have to live in fear of being evicted or struggling to pay rent every month, they can focus on building their lives, advancing in their careers, investing in education, or raising their children without the constant stress of housing insecurity. Secure, affordable housing is a foundation for personal and family stability. And when a government ensures that this is available for all, it creates a more stable society overall. People are healthier, happier, and more engaged in the world around them when their most basic need, a roof over their heads, isn't dependent on the whims of the market.

Utilities, too, when treated as public goods, lead to greater stability. Think about access to clean water, electricity, and gas. These are things we all rely on to live and function in society. Yet, they're subject to price hikes, market forces, and monopolies in many areas. When public services manage utilities, there's less room for exploitation. Prices are more stable, access is more equal, and the focus is on sustainability and community well-being rather than turning a profit. In regions with limited or privatized water or electricity access, entire communities can suffer, and inequality grows. But when these things are treated as public goods, society is more resilient to crises, and people have a greater sense of security.

It's the same with education. When education is treated as a public good, everyone has the chance to succeed, not just those who can afford expensive tuition or private schooling. Education is the key to breaking cycles of poverty and inequality. Yet, we've allowed it to become increasingly privatized and stratified. Let's make education universally accessible and free, like in many Scandinavian countries. We will level the playing field for everyone. People would have the opportunity to learn, innovate, and contribute to society in ways they might not have been able to if education were limited by their family's financial situation.

This would lead to a more educated, equitable workforce, fewer social divides, and stronger communities.

The argument against treating these things as public goods often comes from the idea that government intervention is inefficient or overreaching. But I'd argue that it's much more inefficient to have a fragmented system that leaves people without access to what they need, especially when private companies decide who gets access based on their ability to pay. A society where healthcare, education, housing, and utilities are privatized is inherently unequal, where only the wealthiest can fully participate in society, and the rest are left to scramble. Treating these things as public goods creates a foundation of fairness, equality, and stability. And let's not forget that treating these services as public goods doesn't mean we eliminate the private sector. It just means everyone has a right to them, regardless of their economic situation.

So, why is it considered radical to want this for everyone? It's not radical. It's what leads to a fairer, more just society where everyone has the chance to succeed. It's about recognizing that no one should be left behind simply because they don't have the resources to pay for what they need to survive. Suppose we really want to build a stronger, more stable country. In that case, we need to stop seeing basic amenities as privileges for the few and start treating them as the public goods they are. This is common sense; it's just time we start embracing it.

# Evidence-Based Governance

It's difficult for me to conceive that advocating for evidence-based governance is seen as radical or overly idealistic. All we're talking about is making decisions based on what actually works, using data and rigorous testing to create policies that benefit society. Why is that such a controversial or "extreme" idea? Isn't the point of governance to improve people's lives and create a society that works for everyone? Yet, repeatedly, we see policies being pushed forward based on ideology, political expediency, or sheer guesswork rather than on proven outcomes. The idea that we should strive for policies tested for social welfare seems like basic common sense, but somehow, it's become an uphill battle just to make that case.

Part of the reason it's so hard to advocate for evidence-based governance is because of how deeply entrenched our political systems are in ideology and partisanship. Politics is often about winning arguments, scoring points, and holding onto power rather than finding solutions that work for people. When you bring up evidence-based policies, it's almost like you're threatening the status quo. Those in power may not want to be held accountable to data or research that shows their policies aren't working. There's this fear that if we look too closely at the evidence, we'll have to confront uncomfortable truths or challenge long-held beliefs. That's why we get policies that are half-baked or not thoroughly thought through; they're often driven more by political goals than by actual need or evidence. It's easier to stick with what's familiar, even if it's not working, than to face the challenging process of rethinking things based on evidence.

Then there's the reality that rigorous testing and evaluation take time and money. In a system obsessed with short-term results and quick fixes, implementing a new policy and waiting to see how it plays out can seem like a luxury. But that's precisely what we need if we build policies that improve people's lives in the long run. It's easy to come up with ideas for what "should" work, but what really matters is what does work. Plenty of well-meaning policies fail because they were never adequately tested or didn't account for the complexities of real-world implementation. If we're serious about social welfare, we need to be just as serious about testing policies and measuring their effectiveness before rolling them out on a larger scale.

Another challenge is the resistance to change. People often get caught up in the notion that things should be done how they've always been. Challenging existing systems is uncomfortable, even when the evidence shows those systems aren't serving the people they're meant to. This deeply ingrained belief is that if something is part of the "system," it must be correct or good enough. But that kind of thinking ignores that many of our policies, especially in healthcare, housing, and education, are broken or inefficient. If we want to make progress, we need to move past the belief that "the way things are" is the best way and instead focus on what the evidence says will improve outcomes.

Finally, there's a lack of public understanding of how evidence-based governance works. Most people aren't familiar with the process of policy testing or the importance of rigorous evaluation, making it harder to push for such an approach. Suppose you're constantly hearing political leaders talk about vague promises and ideas. In that case, getting caught up in the rhetoric is easier than demanding more substantial, evidence-driven policies. But this is the problem with so much of the political discourse today; it's based on slogans and sound bites, not on data or facts. We need to change that mindset and start insisting on policies built on evidence, tested for effectiveness, and designed with real-world outcomes in mind. Advocating for evidence-based governance shouldn't be considered "radical." It's simply about being smart and practical in approaching policy. It's about ensuring we're working to improve people's lives rather than sticking with ideas because they're familiar or politically convenient. Suppose we want to build a better society. In that case, we must embrace the idea that policies should be tested, evaluated, and grounded in reality, not just ideology. That should be the bare minimum for any government serious about its people's welfare. So, why is it so hard to advocate for this? I think it's because it challenges the political norms that keep things as they are. But that's precisely why we need to keep pushing for it. It's time we demand policies that work, not just those that make us feel or look good.

# Science And Data Should Guide Policies

It's wildly baffling that advocating for policies based on science and data rather than ideological debates is considered radical or extremist. Why is it considered extreme to want decisions grounded in evidence that we know will work for society? We hear about the latest scientific findings on climate change, healthcare, education, or poverty every day. However, when it comes to policy, we're still too often stuck in the muck of political ideology. For some, it feels more important to hold onto an ideological position than to face the truth about what science and data tell us. That's what makes me "radical" in some eyes because I want to cut through the noise of ideological warfare and put the well-being of society first, using what we know works.

Science and data aren't perfect, but they're the best tools to understand the world around us. When we make decisions based on scientific research, we remove a lot of the guesswork and emotional baggage that tends to cloud political debates. For example, when we talk about climate change, it's not just some abstract concept; it's based on decades of data and research that show us the apparent trajectory of what will happen if we don't act. So why, in the face of this, are there still debates about whether climate change is real or whether we should do something about it? It's not about ideology; it's about looking at the data and recognizing the problem for what it is. But the moment you start saying that we need to address climate change based on evidence, you're branded as an extremist, someone who's pushing for sweeping changes without consideration for the economy or the political fallout. Yet, the truth is, those who deny the science are extreme; they're ignoring the genuine facts that show us the harm of inaction.

It's the same with issues like healthcare. Studies and global comparisons show that universal healthcare leads to better outcomes. Countries with universal healthcare systems consistently outperform those without when it comes to public health. The data is clear. But somehow, arguing for healthcare as a human right, something that should be universally accessible, is seen as a radical left-wing stance. It's considered extreme to suggest that we should organize our society based on what works rather than allowing private entities to profit from people's health. In my view, the radical part is the system we currently have, which prioritizes profits over people's well-being. But when you propose evidence-based policies that aim to make healthcare a public good, you're suddenly the extremist. It's frustrating because all we're asking for is a system that considers the evidence.

The same can be said about education. A growing body of research shows that early childhood education, for example, is a determinant of lifelong success. Yet, when I argue that we should invest more in universal early education, the response from some circles is that it's too expensive or too big a shift. But it's already proven to save money in the long run through better health outcomes, lower crime rates, and higher productivity. The data shows this clearly, but rather than debating the evidence, we're still fighting over political ideology. Why is it that advocating for policies that help people thrive is considered radical when all it's based on is a simple understanding of the facts?

The problem is that ideology often gets in the way of the facts. When political debates are driven by party lines and entrenched beliefs, the science and data can easily get lost in the noise. For example, the idea that capitalism should be left unregulated, even when data shows that unregulated capitalism leads to massive inequality and environmental harm, is an ideological stance, not a rational conclusion based on evidence. But suggesting that we should regulate capitalism to address these problems? Now you're the radical. The extreme one. It's a strange irony that the people who are calling for more regulation to correct the flaws of an unregulated system are often the ones who are labelled as "extreme." In contrast, despite overwhelming evidence of its harms, those defending a broken system are somehow considered the mainstream.

I'm not arguing for a world where science and data are the only things that matter. Of course, human experience, ethics, and values play a role in shaping policy. However, we risk doing harm when we make policies based on ideology alone, without considering what the evidence tells us. It's radical to want to prioritize what's good for society based on proven methods rather than perpetuate systems that we know aren't working. It's radical to believe that we should solve problems with the tools that work, not just those that keep certain power structures in place. What's genuinely extreme is sticking to outdated, ineffective policies because they align with a particular ideology, even when the data shows they do more harm than good.

It seems that true radicalism lies in ignoring the evidence and continuing to let ideology drive policy. Advocating for science-based policies is not extreme; it's common sense. However, as long as we allow political and economic ideologies to dominate the conversation, those who push for evidence-based change will continue to be labelled as radicals. I guess that's just the cost of bringing reason, data, and common sense to a system that's often more interested in preserving power than improving lives.

# Universal Education And Healthcare

It honestly blows my mind that advocating for universal education and healthcare is considered radical. These are things that every society should have, and we already know from countless studies and examples worldwide that they're essential to reducing inequality and maximizing productivity. How is it extreme to argue that everyone should have access to quality education and healthcare, regardless of income or background? These aren't just lofty ideals but practical solutions to some of our most pressing problems. Yet somehow, in the eyes of many, suggesting that we make these things universal is seen as a dangerous, radical proposal.

Let's talk about education for a minute. We know that access to quality education is one of the most effective ways to break the cycle of poverty and inequality. When educated, people are more likely to contribute to the economy, lead healthier lives, and participate actively in society. However, the reality is that too many people are denied this opportunity simply because of their economic circumstances. Those who can't afford private schooling or access to higher education are often stuck with fewer opportunities, and that perpetuates the inequality we see today. Universal education isn't just some pipe dream; it's a proven way to level the playing field. And yet, every time we talk about universal education, there's a pushback from those who think it's too costly or unrealistic. But breaking it down, the benefits far outweigh the costs. Educated populations lead to more innovation, better healthcare, and stronger economies.

Isn't that something we should be striving for? How is it radical to want to give every person the chance to learn and thrive?

The same logic applies to healthcare. It's not radical to say that health should be a human right. It's essential for everyone's well-being, and, in the long run, it saves money. Healthier people are more productive, miss fewer work days, and contribute more to society. And yet, we're still stuck in this ideological debate about whether people deserve access to healthcare based on their ability to pay. How is it radical to want a system where healthcare is not a commodity but a right? Countries with universal healthcare systems have proven that universal coverage leads to better health outcomes, lower costs, and a healthier, more productive population. The evidence is clear, and yet, somehow, proposing that we move towards universal healthcare is still seen as a radical left-wing agenda. It's not radical; it's common sense. We're talking about a system that benefits everyone, from the individual to the economy.

I know there are arguments about the costs of universal education and healthcare. Still, the reality is that these are investments, not expenses. When people are educated and healthy, they can contribute more to society, work better, and even innovate. A healthier, better-educated workforce is a more productive one. So why do we cling to the idea that only those who can afford it should get these benefits? Why is it radical to argue that we should invest in the entire population and ensure everyone has the tools they need to succeed?

And let's not forget that the problem of inequality itself is a significant drain on productivity. When people are locked out of opportunities because they can't afford education or healthcare, society suffers. Inequality leads to worse health outcomes, lower productivity, and more social unrest. Suppose we want to maximize productivity and ensure that everyone has the opportunity to contribute to society. In that case, we need to address the root causes of inequality, things like poor education, inadequate healthcare, and a lack of opportunity. Universal access to education and healthcare tackles those problems head-on. It's not radical to want a society where everyone has access to the resources to help them thrive regardless of their background or income.

So why is it seen as radical to argue for these things? I think it's because we've gotten so used to the idea that only the privileged deserve access to certain benefits. We've bought into the myth that individual success is solely a result of personal effort rather than the systemic advantages that some people are born into. Universal education and healthcare aren't about giving handouts; they're about giving everyone a fair shot at life. They're about creating a system where people can contribute to society to their fullest potential. If that's radical, we may need to rethink what radical means. I'm advocating for a more equitable, productive, and stable society. How can that be a bad thing?

# The Costs For So Called Far-Left 'Extremism'

It's frustrating to hear people argue about the supposed "costs" of far-left policies, especially when those policies are proven to deliver social and economic dividends. The whole narrative that universal education, healthcare, and other public services are too expensive doesn't hold water when you look at the bigger picture. The upfront costs can seem daunting, but the long-term benefits far outweigh them. We already know that investing in education and healthcare creates healthier, more productive societies. So why are the very people advocating for these services, which pay dividends not only to individuals but to society as a whole, accused of being radicals or extremists? It's as if the moment you suggest making basic needs accessible to everyone, you're automatically branded as a burden on the economy when, in fact, the opposite is true.

Take healthcare as an example. The argument that universal healthcare is too costly ignores the reality of what we're spending now under a system where private companies profit from people's illnesses. The U.S., for example, spends more per capita on healthcare than any other country. Yet, its system leaves millions without adequate coverage. If we were to move towards a public healthcare model, sure, we'd be investing more upfront, but we'd also see massive savings in the long run. Healthier populations lead to lower overall healthcare costs, reduced absenteeism from work, and fewer people relying on emergency services. These aren't just theories but proven facts in countries with universal healthcare. Universal healthcare's social and economic dividends are clear: better public health outcomes, reduced inequality, and a more productive workforce. But when you argue for this, it's often dismissed as "extremist" because it challenges the status quo, which is built on private profit rather than public welfare.

The same goes for education. We know that the cost of not investing in education is far greater than the cost of providing quality education for all. Without universal education, we continue to perpetuate cycles of poverty and inequality. People who lack education are less likely to contribute to the economy, are more likely to rely on social services, and are more likely to suffer from poor health outcomes. Conversely, when everyone has access to quality education, society benefits, there's lower crime, better health, and a more skilled workforce. Again, these aren't just abstract ideas. Countries with better education systems outperform those without regarding quality of life and economic productivity. So why is it so radical to argue for these investments when they literally pay off in terms of social stability and economic growth?

Then there's the argument about universal housing, another so-called "far-left" policy that gets demonized. If you provide people with stable housing, you're not just offering them a roof over their heads but investing in their potential to contribute to society. Homelessness costs society a great deal, from increased healthcare needs to law enforcement expenses. Affordable housing benefits those living in those homes and society by reducing those long-term costs. When people have a stable place to live, they're healthier, more productive, and more likely to contribute positively to their communities. So why is it considered extreme to advocate for this? It's not extreme, it's practical. It's an investment that pays dividends in the form of a more stable, productive, and healthier society.

The narrative that far-left policies are "too expensive" is built on the idea that investing in the social safety net somehow deters the economy, when the opposite is true. In fact, these policies contribute to a more resilient economy by reducing inequality, increasing productivity, and improving public health. But because these solutions challenge the dominant capitalist model, they're often dismissed as unrealistic or too costly, even though the costs of inaction are much higher. We need to rethink this whole argument. The actual cost lies in maintaining a system prioritizing profit over people, which allows inequality to fester and societal instability to grow. Investing in social services isn't a drain on society; it's a smart economic strategy.

The bottom line is these so-called "radical" policies are anything but. They're rooted in practical solutions that have been proven to work. And yet, the people who advocate for them are often painted as extremists. The real extremism lies in clinging to a system that perpetuates inequality, poor health, and social unrest, all in the name of profit. It's time to stop framing universal services as a burden and start recognizing them for what they are: an investment in the future of our society and economy.

# Global Stability And Democratizing Militarization

It's unbelievable that advocating for global stability and cooperation is considered "extreme" or "unpatriotic." When I say that true patriotism requires pushing for these things, I'm not talking about some naive dream of world peace. I'm talking about the genuine need to shift how we approach militarization and international relations. The idea that our national security and interests can only be protected by a massive, unchecked military buildup or by undermining other nations is not only outdated but incredibly dangerous. If we want to truly protect our country, we must advocate for global stability, cooperation, and democratizing militarization. This doesn't mean disarming; it means ensuring that militaries are not used as tools of oppression or aggression but as forces for peace and protection in a balanced, accountable way.

The current global military dynamic is skewed heavily towards powerful nations, with a lot of military spending going toward advanced weaponry and force projection, often under the guise of "defence." But is it really defence when we're arming ourselves to the teeth while ignoring the structural inequalities and tensions that lead to violence and conflict? True patriotism isn't about mindlessly supporting military spending without asking questions; it's about understanding the global context and our actions impact on others. Suppose we genuinely care about our nation's future. In that case, we need to recognize that global instability affects us all, whether through the ripple effects of war, economic instability, or the environmental degradation caused by conflict. Advocating for a shift towards global cooperation and peacekeeping isn't extreme; it's intelligent. It's the thinking that looks beyond national borders and asks, "How can we all be safer together?"

But democratizing militarization goes even deeper than just calling for peace. It's about ensuring that military power isn't hoarded by a few elites or used to maintain the status quo. If you look at the military-industrial complex, you can see how the current system is designed to benefit corporations and political elites, not ordinary people. This isn't just an American issue; it is a global problem. Militarization too often serves the interests of those who profit from conflict. At the same time, the rest of us are left picking up the pieces. True patriotism, in my eyes, would be about ensuring that our military is used for the proper purposes, under the right circumstances, and with the oversight necessary to prevent misuse. That's not extreme, that's smart, and it's responsible.

When I talk about global stability, I also refer to the need for genuine international cooperation beyond trade deals or military alliances. It's about fostering relationships between nations built on shared peace, human rights, and sustainability values. This doesn't mean giving up our sovereignty or becoming a global doormat. It means recognizing that we're all interconnected, and the only way to build lasting peace is through collaboration, not domination. Patriotism, at its core, is about protecting the well-being of our citizens, and that doesn't happen in isolation. Global instability doesn't respect borders, whether due to climate change, economic disparities, or conflicts between nations. Our safety and security are tied to the planet's health and other nations' stability.

What's genuinely extreme, in my mind, is the idea that militarization is the answer to every problem. Suppose patriotism is about the well-being and future of a nation and its people. In that case, we should be questioning why we invest so much in weapons of war rather than the tools that build peace, resilience, and cooperation. It's extreme to believe that more military power will solve our problems when it's clear that military force often exacerbates the issues we're trying to fix. True patriotism requires a shift in mindset: recognizing that the strength of a nation lies not in its ability to destroy but in its capacity to foster collaboration, address inequality, and promote peace on a global scale.

It's also important to remember that pushing for global stability and cooperation doesn't mean we ignore the needs of our own citizens. In fact, prioritizing international cooperation can actually make us stronger at home. When we work with other nations to address issues like poverty, climate change, and human rights, we create a more stable global environment that benefits everyone, including us. National security isn't just about military readiness; it's about creating a world where diplomacy, cooperation, and shared responsibility are the norms. That's the kind of patriotism I'm talking about, one that looks to the future and asks, "How can we make this world a better place for everyone while also securing a better future for ourselves?"

So when people call me an extremist for suggesting that true patriotism involves advocating for global stability and a more responsible, democratic approach to militarization, it's almost laughable. I'm not advocating for weakness or appeasement. I'm advocating for a more intelligent, more sustainable approach to security that looks beyond just national defence and embraces the kind of cooperation that can bring lasting peace and prosperity to all. That's not extreme. That kind of thinking will protect us in the long run.

# Nations Focusing On Peace And Welfare

It's mind-boggling that the idea of a nation focusing on peace and welfare is considered "radical." Why is it so extreme to imagine a country prioritizing the well-being of its people over military dominance, economic exploitation, or unnecessary competition? A nation that puts peace and welfare at the forefront could become a model for the rest of the world. But somehow, this is seen as a far-left fantasy, a naive utopia, or even worse, some sort of threat. Why is it radical to want a society that focuses on ensuring everyone has access to the basics, education, healthcare, food, housing, and safety? This is the foundation of a stable, thriving nation, and the idea that this is a radical proposal just doesn't make sense.

Think about it for a second. If a country genuinely committed to peace and the welfare of its citizens, investing in public services, social safety nets, and international cooperation, that would be a country with lower crime rates, better health outcomes, less social unrest, and a more productive workforce. This kind of society would naturally attract attention from other nations, not to mention global organizations. It could inspire a shift towards prioritizing human needs over destructive pursuits like endless military spending or economic inequalities. We've seen this work in countries that already focus on peace and social welfare, where high living standards, universal healthcare, and free education are the norm. These countries are often examples of what is possible when the government focuses on improving life for everyone, not just the privileged few.

The idea that focusing on peace and welfare could make a nation a model for others isn't even new. It's been done before, and it works. The Nordic model, for example, has shown the world that you don't need to exploit your population or invest trillions in military power to maintain a strong economy and vibrant society. Countries like Sweden, Denmark, and Norway have some of the highest standards of living in the world, and they've built their success on policies that emphasize social safety nets, equity, and inclusivity. They haven't just survived; they thrive. So why is it that it's considered radical when someone suggests we take inspiration from these models? Why is it so extreme to think that a nation could focus on peace, equality, and the welfare of its people and, in turn, set an example for the rest of the world?

The fact that these ideas are viewed as radical shows how much we've been conditioned to accept the status quo, which often values profit, military power, and competition over the well-being of people. But when you step back and look at it, focusing on peace and welfare isn't just a moral ideal; it's practical. It makes sense from an economic and social perspective. A country that invests in its citizens' welfare will have healthier, more productive people, fewer social issues, and a higher quality of life. That country is strong in ways that go beyond just military might. And isn't that what every nation should strive for? To be strong not just in their ability to dominate but in their ability to foster peace, equality, and prosperity?

It's almost as if the very notion that a country could thrive without war, without inequality, and without the overwhelming presence of corporate interests is so threatening to the powers that be that it has to be labelled as "radical." But why? Why is advocating for peace, fairness, and welfare a threat? Why is it extreme to argue that we could build a model society that other countries could look to as a guide for their development? It's not radical; it's logical. It's common sense. And, frankly, it's the kind of leadership the world needs right now. The model for a prosperous nation shouldn't be one built on oppression, war, or exploitation. It should demonstrate what's possible when we put people first because when we prioritize the welfare of everyone, we all win. That's not radical; it's a vision for a sustainable future.

# Inspiring International Cooperation

Am I crazy that a governance model focused on public welfare could inspire international cooperation? It feels like an idea that should be more common sense than radical thinking. Imagine a world where nations are genuinely focused on the well-being of their people, prioritizing healthcare, education, housing, and environmental sustainability. What if countries were governed not by military strength or economic exploitation but by policies that ensure the basic needs of every citizen are met? This isn't some utopian daydream. This is a practical, logical approach that could actually spark meaningful global cooperation. The potential is enormous, yet somehow, it's still treated as a fringe idea that's too radical to entertain. Why?

If we think about it, the global challenges we face today, climate change, economic inequality, global health crises, mass migration, demand collaboration, not competition. These issues don't respect borders. If one country suffers from a famine or a health crisis, it affects the rest of the world. So, why should we keep approaching these problems with a mindset of isolation and self-interest? A government that centers its policies around the welfare of its people could lead the way toward international cooperation because it would act in the best interests of its citizens and the global community. Take climate change as an example: a country committed to environmental sustainability could work with other nations to reduce emissions, share technology, and invest in green infrastructure. Instead of trying to outdo each other or point fingers, nations could unite over shared goals for a healthier planet.

Governance focused on public welfare could set an example of how international cooperation isn't just a feel-good notion but an essential strategy for survival. Consider how the European Union, for example, has created a framework for cooperation on everything from trade to environmental policy. That model of working together across borders could be expanded to address more global challenges, particularly if the model is built around the idea of prioritizing human rights, social justice, and economic equity. Instead of the traditional, competitive mindset that drives much of international politics today, we could build a system where countries learn from each other, share resources, and solve common problems.

The real question is, why isn't this the norm? Why is it considered crazy or naïve to think that countries could cooperate in ways that actually improve the quality of life for their citizens and for the planet as a whole? It's not like this has never been done before. The world has seen instances of cooperation during times of great crisis, like when countries come together to respond to natural disasters or pandemics. The success of the global vaccine effort during the COVID-19 pandemic is a good example. It wasn't perfect, but cooperation and collaboration in some areas should serve as a reminder that great things can happen when the world comes together for the right reasons. Imagine the possibilities if public welfare-focused governance were the driving force behind that cooperation. Countries could share best practices for reducing inequality, improving education systems, or ensuring universal healthcare.

Of course, this all sounds like a dream to many, and I'm aware that realpolitik and entrenched interests make this kind of collaboration difficult. But that's precisely why pushing the conversation forward is so important. It's not about denying the realities of geopolitics or economic competition; it's about challenging the narrative that our governance systems are locked in a zero-sum game. What if we embraced a more holistic, interconnected governing method acknowledging our shared responsibility for each other's well-being? If nations started adopting policies prioritizing public welfare, they could inspire others to do the same, creating a ripple effect leading to more sustainable and peaceful global relationships. It's not crazy to think this could work; it's the leadership the world desperately needs.

It's tempting to think of cooperation as something that only happens in times of crisis, but what if we could build a world where countries are proactively working together, pooling their resources and knowledge for the common good? That would be a model that could spark not only national transformations but international ones as well. The world is changing fast, and if we continue relying on old, outdated paradigms of competition and isolation, we will only deepen our problems. A public welfare-focused governance model could inspire a new era of global cooperation that prioritizes people over profit, collaboration over conflict, and sustainability over short-term gain. That's not crazy; it's precisely what the world needs to survive and thrive in the years to come.

# Common Human Goals And Global Challenges

How can I be considered radical for thinking governments working together toward common human goals could mitigate global challenges like poverty and climate change? It seems like such a no-brainer to me, yet this idea gets brushed off as extreme or unrealistic. Let's break it down: if we genuinely acknowledged that humanity shares everyday needs and struggles, wouldn't it make sense for governments to put their heads together and tackle global issues like poverty, inequality, and environmental destruction collectively? Instead, we continue to perpetuate this idea that nations need to work against each other to survive and that cooperation is some utopian dream. But suppose governments came together to ensure human flourishing by addressing climate change, ending poverty, and improving access to basic needs. In that case, that's a solid foundation for a safer, more sustainable world.

Just think about the scale of the challenges we face. Climate change, global poverty, healthcare access, and mass displacement are not problems any country can solve alone. They're interconnected, and they require a global response. So why is it radical to suggest that countries could work together to address these issues? We already see examples of international cooperation, albeit often too small or fragmented. For instance, the Paris Agreement on climate change is a step in the right direction, even though it's far from enough. But what if this type of international coordination wasn't just an exception but the rule? What if we had a global commitment to fight poverty, protect the environment, and improve health outcomes? That wouldn't be radical, it would be common sense.

When we talk about addressing poverty, it's clear that no country can be prosperous in isolation. The wealth disparity between the Global North and South is staggering, and no amount of charity can truly fix it. Governments must work together to create sustainable systems that lift people out of poverty, provide equitable access to education, and ensure that resources are distributed more fairly. Climate change is another example. This is not a localized issue; the planet's ecosystems don't care about borders. If the Global South suffers from the effects of climate change, it will ripple through the entire world, including the wealthier nations. Tackling these global issues requires the kind of cooperation and shared vision I'm talking about: governments aligning their goals around the human good, not just national interests.

But, somehow, this gets framed as "radical." Why? Because it challenges the status quo. It disrupts the idea that each nation has to fend for itself and that competition is the ultimate driver of success. The truth is that, in a globally connected world, cooperation is the most effective way to achieve lasting change. If we get past the idea that countries have to protect their interests above all else, we could start to focus on the shared human goals that would lead to peace, prosperity, and environmental sustainability. It's not a radical vision; it's a necessary one.

So, why is it considered extreme to think governments should collaborate to fight global issues? It's not like it's a pipe dream. Let's think about the scale of the global crises we face: climate change, inequality, and resource depletion. We don't have time to continue the old isolation and competition paradigm. The issues are global, so the responses must also be global. Whether we like it or not, the world is interconnected, and no country can escape the impacts of international problems. Tackling them collectively isn't radical; it's the only way forward.

The more I think about it, the more it frustrates me how something as logical as international cooperation is seen as radical or naive. We've seen, time and time again, that when countries come together, they can make huge strides, whether it's in technology, trade, or healthcare. So why, when it comes to the most urgent issues facing humanity, is it so hard to envision a world where governments are working together, not against each other? It doesn't make sense that calling for collaboration to address climate change or poverty is framed as "too extreme." It's the opposite: it's the pragmatic, sensible approach. It's about time we stopped thinking of ourselves as separate nations competing for survival and started recognizing that we all share this planet and its challenges. Only then can we create a future that works for everyone.

# Compassion, Equity, And Responsibility

Why am I considered an "extremist" for having a vision that, while ambitious, is rooted in compassion, equity, and responsibility? It's honestly baffling. When you propose a future where people are treated with dignity, where wealth is redistributed to create more equality, and where governments act as responsible stewards of resources for the benefit of all, you get labelled as extreme. But isn't that the kind of world we should be striving for? A world where everyone has access to basic needs like healthcare and education, a safe place to live, and where we can take care of our environment for future generations? This isn't a fantasy or a utopia; it's a vision based on human decency and sound, evidence-backed principles. It's rooted in the idea that we must look out for one another and share in the abundance this planet can provide. So, why is it considered radical to care about these things? Why is it extremist to say we should be doing better?

At the heart of this vision is compassion. Being compassionate is one of the things that makes my ideas seem "extreme." What's extreme about wanting to build a society where no one has to suffer because of a lack of access to food, shelter, or healthcare? What's radical about saying we should help those struggling rather than disregard their pain? I look around, and it's clear that some people are falling through the cracks, whether it's due to inequality, lack of healthcare, or the environmental challenges we face. I'm not proposing something out of the realm of possibility. I'm proposing policies and ideas grounded in the understanding that we are all part of the same human family, and we have an ethical duty to ensure that everyone can live a life of dignity and opportunity.

Then, there's the idea of equity. How is advocating for fairness and equal access to resources extreme? Isn't the point of a society to ensure that everyone has a fair shot? It's frustrating to see the word "equity" twisted into something negative when, at its core, it's simply about making sure that no one is left behind because of the circumstances of their birth. Whether it's access to quality education, a living wage, or decent healthcare, there's no reason these should be privileges for the few rather than rights for all. And yet, here I am, being called extreme for imagining a world where these things are universally accessible. But what could be more reasonable than wanting to level the playing field so that everyone, regardless of background or social status, has the same opportunities to succeed?

The final piece of my vision is responsibility, not just on an individual level but on a systemic level. It's about holding governments, corporations, and institutions accountable for their actions' impact on people and the planet. For example, why should it be radical to demand that corporations be responsible for their environmental footprint or that governments be accountable for ensuring citizens' welfare? Why is it extreme to expect the people in charge of large-scale systems to act with the best interests of society in mind? The argument against responsibility usually comes down to the desire to protect profits or power, but at some point, we must ask ourselves: at what cost? How long can we keep allowing corporations to prioritize their bottom line over the well-being of the population and the planet? It doesn't seem extreme to me to think that responsibility should be a core value of leadership in a world as interconnected as ours.

I don't think my vision is extreme, but it's ambitious. That could be what freaks people out: ambition. The idea that we could build a world where compassion, equity, and responsibility aren't just ideals but the foundation of how we organize society that'sis a powerful vision. And sure, it might be challenging to get there, but shouldn't we be aiming for significant, transformative changes that improve life for everyone? Isn't that the vision that should be celebrated rather than ridiculed? It's not extreme to want better for the world; it's realistic. If anything, it's radical to cling to the status quo when the current system is failing so many people. So, if being an "extremist" means advocating for a world built on compassion, equity, and responsibility, then maybe I'm an extremist. Still, I'll wear that label with pride because I genuinely believe that's the world we need.

# Why Am I The 'Extremist'?

Can someone explain to me how I'm somehow seen as a far-left "extremist" for holding views that are reasonable, rational, practical, sustainable, and, honestly, evidence-based? When did advocating for basic human decency and a responsible social contract become controversial? We're at this strange point where the idea that the government should be held accountable for the welfare of its citizens or that the economy should serve the people rather than the other way around is seen as a radical departure from reality. But these are common-sense principles, ideas that prioritize sustainability, long-term planning, and the well-being of everyone, not just those with wealth and influence. And yet, here we are in a world where equitable public healthcare, education, and fair wages are treated like an impossible fantasy. I have to wonder how we got here.

We've forgotten what the social contract is supposed to be about. At its core, a social contract should ensure that every citizen has a fair chance to live a good life, with access to basic necessities and the ability to contribute meaningfully to society. This isn't a pie-in-the-sky ideal; it's the foundation of responsible citizenship and a healthy nation. Yet, in today's world, when I argue that governments should fulfill their part of this contract by ensuring healthcare, education, and protections for the environment, I'm labelled as extreme. Since when has it been ridiculous to expect a system that's fair, responsible, and designed for the good of everyone? If anything, what's genuinely irrational is a system where public goods are privatized, where profits are prioritized over people, and where there's an endless pursuit of growth without regard for sustainability. It's extreme to think we can ignore these responsibilities and still expect a stable society.

Let's talk about practicality. Advocating for universal healthcare, accessible education, and regulated markets isn't a revolutionary call to arms; it's based on practical experience and evidence. Countries with these systems already show better health outcomes, lower levels of poverty, and higher overall well-being. Why should we ignore data that tells us this approach works? Somehow, I'm an "extremist" for pointing to decades of studies to say that policies rooted in evidence should shape how we run our societies. The truth is, these ideas aren't radical and are not new; they're just logical. If something is proven to work and improve lives, shouldn't we be implementing it? It's mystifying that evidence-based policy, essentially common sense, is treated with suspicion while decisions driven by ideology or corporate interests are normalized.

Even sustainability, which should be non-negotiable by now, gets me labelled a dreamer. It shouldn't be extreme to suggest that our policies and practices need to consider the future and that we shouldn't deplete resources, destroy ecosystems, or poison the planet. And yet, advocating for environmental responsibility is somehow seen as fringe. This planet is our only home, and the science is clear that we're pushing it to the brink. To me, it's insanity not to act, to pretend we can continue business as usual while ignoring the harm we're causing. When I call for sustainable practices, I'm calling for survival, for policies that give us a shot at a livable future. How is that extreme?

I think we've allowed the concept of "responsible citizenship" to be hijacked by those who profit from the current system. A responsible social contract should prioritize the well-being of all citizens, but we've reached a point where corporate interests and individual wealth are often put above public welfare. When I say that we need to rethink our priorities and reinvest in public goods and services, I'm not pushing for some utopian ideal; I'm asking for a balanced, functional society. The social contract should mean everyone contributes, benefits, and is protected. That's not radical; it's what keeps a nation healthy. But now, even asking for this is seen as naive or idealistic.

I'm left wondering how we reached a place where expecting rational, sustainable policies for the collective good is viewed as an "extreme" stance. It's not ridiculous to believe in equity, sustainability, and accountability; it's what responsible governance should be. We shouldn't be measuring ideas by how much they protect wealth or privilege but by how much they protect and uplift all people. Yet, somehow, we've allowed the standards for responsible, fair governance to drift so far that it now feels like common sense has been painted as radical.